A C

Guide to

SELF-ESTEEM

RUSSELL ABATA, C.SS.R., S.T.D.

Liguori
ONE LIGUORI DRIVE
LIGUORI MO 63057-9999

Imprimi Potest:
Richard Thibodeau, C.Ss.R.
Provincial, Denver Province
The Redemptorists

ISBN 0-7648-0472-3
Library of Congress Catalog Card Number: 99-71462

Scripture quotations are from the *New Revised Standard Version of the Bible*, © 1989 by the Division of Christian Education of the National Council of the Churches of Christ in the USA. Used with permission. All rights reserved.

This booklet was previously published under the title *Self-Esteem: Key to Happiness*, © 1994, Liguori Publications.

To order, call 1-800-325-9521
http://www.liguori.org

Cover design by Jamie Wyatt

CONTENTS

PREFACE

Most people want to be happy. Indeed, they spend most of their time and effort seeking the things they believe will help them be happy. This booklet is about a vitally important key to human happiness: self-esteem. How others esteem you and, more important, how you esteem yourself play a major part in how happy you are.

In examining the subject of self-esteem, we will consider first how other people can influence your self-esteem. It can be an enormous, even overwhelming influence. Second, we will look at the part your own feelings play in your judgments about yourself. If you are not fully aware of them, your own feelings can be the deciding factor in your sense of self-worth.

Our third consideration will be about you—the real, mature, whole you that *should* be the basis of your self-esteem. Your real self is like the rock foundation Jesus speaks about in the Sermon on the Mount. (See Matthew 7:24.) It is like the pearl of great price the merchant searched for. (See Matthew 13:45-46.) When you discover this real you and make it the basis of your self-esteem, you have already begun to be happy. This is not simply a statement or a promise. It is a guarantee.

1. THE IMAGINARY YOU

If you are like most people, how you esteem yourself depends on how others esteem you. If others approve of the things you are doing, you feel good about yourself. If they do not approve, you feel down on yourself. It is not difficult to understand why this happens. From the very beginning, other people have played important roles in your life. Your being and well-being has depended on them. So why should your judgment about your worth not depend on them, especially if they have desired good for you?

While it is not difficult to understand why other people's opinions influence your judgments about your own worth, just why they continue to wield so much power over your self-image is a little more difficult to grasp. Many of the people whose judgments continue to influence you are absent, even dead. Yet the tapes they recorded in your head are still playing: "Feel this. Do not feel that. Think this. Do not think that. Do this. Do not do that."

If you do exactly as the recordings say, you feel safe. You feel good about yourself. If you do not do exactly what they say, you feel awful, as if you are not safe. Are these dos and don'ts in your head merely voices? No, they also form a picture. Your creative imagination has pasted all that others want you to be into a picture. This picture that you carry in your memory lets you know when you are or are not living up to the expectations of others.

Your Image

This picture your imagination has put together is often called *the imagined you* or *the image you* or simply your *image*. This image is made up of all the things the important people in your life—your parents, teachers, religious leaders, peers, and society leaders—say you must be to be accepted.

What is this picture like? For most people, it depends on qualities such as being good, smart, honest, holy, helpful, loyal and successful. At times, it can be a very lofty picture of an idealized you.

This picture we receive from others is often called the "ego." People commonly speak about their own ego or the ego of others: "She did not have enough ego to be successful at her job." Very often the ego spoken of is one that is too lofty or too idealized. If someone falls on his face because he assumed airs of importance, people may say, "His ego was too big." If people worry over whom to invite to a restricted party, they have to be concerned about egos being hurt—those not invited and their own for not inviting them.

Ego is the Latin word for our pronoun *I*. Because so many people identify the picture put together by their imaginations as being who they really are or should be, the picture becomes their *I*. They look to it to direct them in all aspects of their lives.

An Old Confusion

If you have identified the picture formed by your imagination as being who you really are, you are not alone in your confusion. Many others think this way. In fact, this confusion is directly related to our use of the word *person*.

Ordinarily, to be called one's own person is considered a high compliment. It indicates that the individual so named is real, authentic. Strangely, however, this is the opposite of its original meaning.

The word *person* comes from the Latin word *persona*, which means "to wear a mask" or "to be a character in a play." It was recognized centuries ago that for most people becoming a person

7

means to wear a mask or to become like an actor or actress in a play. In so doing, they mask what would be displeasing and follow a script that would be pleasing to others. That is what it means to be a *person*.

Today, most of us still confuse our images or egos with our real selves. We mask what is not acceptable and try to act the part of what is acceptable. In the areas of cleanliness, manners, relationships, and business dealings there is a set of dos and don'ts on how we should and should not conduct ourselves. People of the same background have most of the same dos and don'ts. We see this with the Pharisees in Jesus' time, and we still see it in modern society.

Jesus spent a good part of the Sermon on the Mount denouncing the hypocrisy of those who, like the Pharisees, did things, even good things, just for show. He warned them to "beware of practicing your piety before others in order to be seen by them; for then you have no reward from your Father in heaven" (Matthew 6:1).

In contemporary society, acting solely from image is so commonplace that for some it dictates the clothes they wear and the way they act for fear of rejection.

CONSCIENCE

Another name often given to this picture put together by our imaginations is *conscience*. For most people, their image or ego is their conscience. It tells them what is morally acceptable and what is not. It gives them the verdict of guilty or not guilty, depending on whether or not they live up to its dictates.

This kind of conscience, based on the dos and don'ts of others, was given at a very early age. Many of its dictates have never changed. For the person with this kind of conscience, following these dos and don'ts becomes more important than understanding why a thing is right or wrong. Since it is a conscience concerned with being safe or unsafe, it often goes overboard to be safe. It is a rewarding/punishing conscience.

In many ways, it is a child's conscience. It applies only what it has learned from others; it has not digested and analyzed these orders received from others.

Usually, it is a conscience that bases its verdict on the good or bad consequences of an act. If something turns out badly, it screams out guilt. If something turns out good, it praises. For many, it is the "voice of God." Although it was formed by humans, it carries the authority of God.

SEVERAL NAMES, ONE REALITY

Although *image, ego,* and many times *conscience* all refer to the picture your imagination has formed to win the approval of others, in this booklet I will usually refer to this picture as the *image you* or *your image.* I want to impress on you that what we are considering is not a real person. It is an *it.* It is a product of your imagination.

It will be helpful here to point out how important this image you is to your life. Depending on how the dos and don'ts were imposed and depending on how you received them and put them together, your image has important potential for both good and bad. It can add to or take away so much from your life. After we consider its positive and negative potential, we will consider the effects your image has on your self-esteem and confidence.

POSITIVE POTENTIAL

An image or ego of the proper size—neither too small nor too big—can be of value in many areas of your life. One of these is the social area—getting along with people. Your ego tells you what is and what is not acceptable to others.

Another important area where your image is helpful is in your individual development. Other people provide you with instant knowledge about many things. All you have to do is to copy and memorize what you were told or shown. You have taken advantage of this in many ways, perhaps without realizing it.

- How would you know how to communicate with others if you had not been taught the use of language?
- How would you enjoy the advances of science if others did not achieve and share their achievements with you?

- How would you learn the lessons of history if others did not record them and share them with you?
- How would you know about proper moral conduct if others had not worked them out and given them to you?
- How would you approach God and religion if others did not preserve, develop, and share their experiences and learning with you?

In these and other areas, it is obvious that a well-formed image contributes to your well-being. To have to learn everything by yourself, from your own experience, would take too long and would expose you to dangers that you would very likely not survive. A healthy image, therefore, is valuable as a consultant or reference book. It is like having a good, intelligent parent or teacher in your head.

THE NEGATIVE SIDE

An unrealistic, overidealistic image or ego is not only a burden and a source of trouble, it can be a disaster, playing havoc in countless ways. In the important social area of relating to others, it can make you vulnerable to the most ridiculous fears. Do you look all right? Is your nose too big? Is your body too tall, too small, too heavy, too thin? Did you say the right things? Will they think you're stupid because of something you said or did not say? Do you wear the right clothes? Were you overdressed or underdressed for the party? Do you walk the right way? Do you hold your body too erect, too proud, too slouched, too humble?

If the image you is too big, it can give you both a "superiority" and an "inferiority" complex. You have the desperate need to live up to all of the ideals you have imagined are important. You are a perfectionist. This is the superiority part.

Most of the time, though, you do not have the ability to live up to such superior qualities. You always or often come away with a bad report card of your performance. You feel humiliated. This is the inferiority part.

If you show off the superiority part, you come across as proud, self-righteous, judgmental, critical, and isolated. If you dwell on the inferiority part, you come across as shy, quiet, a doormat, a shadow, lacking in confidence. From the standpoint of conscience, you can become worried over the slightest moral decision or transgression. You can become so scrupulous that you need the constant reassurance of authority figures to convince you that you are safe.

Trying to live up to an exaggerated image or ego, you can become weary and burned out physically, emotionally, and spiritually. Everything has gone for show and to prove that you are good, smart, holy, successful. On the inside, however, little or nothing is left. As you can see, such an image spells trouble. It is especially bad news when it comes to the important area of self-esteem.

IMAGE AND YOUR SELF-ESTEEM

If you are one of those people who tallies your self-esteem and worth on the basis of the acceptance or nonacceptance of others, you can see how important your image is.

Your image tells you what is acceptable or nonacceptable to others. Even if others are not actually present to see what you are doing, they continue to operate in you by way of your image. Your image will echo their praise and make you feel worthwhile if you do what they would approve of. At those times your self-esteem skyrockets.

By the same token, your image will condemn you and make you feel worthless if you do something others would not approve of. The lurking feeling is that "if they knew, they would not approve of me." That lurking feeling can often plunge your self-esteem into bankruptcy. Whether you are aware of it or not, your image serves four purposes.

1. It tells you what the "big" people—parents, teachers, religious, and societal leaders—want of you.
2. It gives you a report card on how well you have lived up to what those people want.

3. It tells you what your peers want of you.
4. It gives you a report card on how well you have lived up to what your peers want.

It is the two report cards that are so important to your self-esteem. They are like the reviews actors and actresses depend on to know how well they performed, or at least how the critics viewed their performances. If the reviews are good, the actors and actresses feel good. If the reviews are bad, they feel bad.

If your report cards are good, your self-esteem is high. You have great confidence. You feel great. You feel you can manage your world. If your report cards are bad, your self-esteem is low. You have no confidence. You can dwell so much on what you do not have, you feel like you are nothing. You feel terrible. In some cases, death seems preferable to life.

This is where you find yourself if you base your self-esteem on others. Depending on how you live up to your image, you can feel high on yourself or down on yourself.

YOUR IMAGE AT WORK

Because your image or ego can have such awesome power over you, it is important to be aware of its presence, activities, and influences on your life. It is not always easy to detect its workings within you. Your image has become such a steady part of you, you could mistake it for your real self. In the next few sections, we will describe some ways to know when your image is at work and perhaps dominating you.

The nervous smile or laugh

When we fail to know or do something as perfectly as our image says we should, we become embarrassed. We are filled with shame, and this shame will usually spill over into a nervous smile or laugh. This quick, nervous smile or laugh covers up what we are really feeling. In our embarrassment, we would rather cry or get angry, but that is not acceptable. Instead, with our smile or laughter, it is as if we are saying, "I will show you that what is happening is not bothering me."

This nervous reaction happens automatically. If you want to try a relatively harmless experiment, ask someone you know, "How much is 37 multiplied by 37?" Most likely, she will smile nervously. If you follow up with "You really don't know the answer, do you?" she will probably laugh, shrug her shoulders, and perhaps perform some other bodily reaction of uneasiness. This is more likely to happen if others are present. You are embarrassing her. What would her math teachers think of her for not knowing the answer?

I sometimes put this question to a group. Off the top of their heads, no one knows the answer. The one I call on smiles nervously, smirks, and then laughs. It is sad to see the power we give to others. My question implies that there is something wrong with the person if he does not know the answer. He begins to feel stupid. Actually, of course, I do not know the answer myself.

The same embarrassed reaction to a damaged image can happen to a woman who falls on a dance floor. She is more concerned with how she looks than whether she is hurt. She is embarrassed because she has been clumsy. She laughs and tries to make light of it. She does not want anyone making a big fuss over her.

Extreme criticism of self and others

We find fault with ourselves because we cannot live up to the perfect image in our heads. This perfect image beats up on us and scolds us as if we were children: "You never do anything right. You are so stupid."

To avoid criticism from our image, we might refer to our faults in the second person. Instead of saying, "I did this stupid thing," we prefer to soften the damage to our image by saying, "You know, you do stupid things when you are in a hurry and you are busy with a number of things. No one is perfect."

By putting ourselves in a group where others are doing the same or worse, we do not appear so bad. Most gossip probably stems from talking about others' faults so the one revealing them does not look so bad. Obviously, this tendency is destructive to self-identity. To identify with everyone else is to lack a personal identity.

When we find excessive fault with others, we are probably judging them against our perfect self-image. Those who fail to do what our image says should be done are at fault. Severe criticism of others comes from a projection of our own faults.

When the image appears on a movie screen, it is easy to forget that it is actually coming from the film in the projector. When we severely criticize another, the fault that is bothering us is most likely inside ourselves. The person under attack is like the movie screen. He may possess the fault to some degree, but his fault is not the real problem. The real problem is that we are not ready or able to see or accept the fault inside ourselves. Our image would punish us too severely with shame and guilt for having it. So we tell ourselves and others that the fault is in the other person.

Pointing fingers

A simple way to illustrate how projecting works is to point an accusing finger at someone. Look at your hand. While you point one finger at another, you are pointing three back at yourself. You probably have the same fault as bad, even worse, than the other.

Jesus points this out vividly when he says, "Why do you see the speck in your neighbor's eye, but do not notice the log in your own eye?…You hypocrite, first take the log out of your own eye, and then you will see clearly to take the speck out of your neighbor's eye" (Matthew 7:3-5). As you might suspect, being aware of this tendency can help you cut down on your fault-finding in others. It can also help you discover hard-to-accept truths about yourself. This self discovery can be a source of self growth. Above all, it can help you detect how much your image is at work inside you.

A POWERFUL INFLUENCE

A healthy image can supply you with valuable assistance for healthy living. An unhealthy image can fill you with tension and rob you of your heart and soul.

In my own life, in dealing with something as insignificant as going prematurely bald, I can testify to the discomfort and tension my image caused me.

Once upon a time, I had beautiful curly hair. Kids on the block wanted to know if I got it from eating the crusts of bread. I guess they figured the curled-up crusts were responsible for the curl in my hair. Then my hair became wavy. In my late twenties, it waved good-bye.

For a long time, my hair was imported. The few strands I had were brought over from the other side. I wore a hat constantly to make sure an ill wind did not blow those few strands back over to the side of their origin.

I can laugh at myself now that I realize where the embarrassment and tension I experienced came from, but it was not always that way. Nor is it that way for those who do not realize what a disservice their image can do them. The same holds true for people who are very short, uneducated, or poorly dressed. Their image pounces on and devours these perceived imperfections and comes up with incredible shame.

If you are under a great deal of stress, it might help to refer to this chapter many times. It could point out some of the source of your stress: you are trying too hard to please or to avoid displeasing others.

A BETTER SELF-IMAGE

In concluding this chapter I want to consider an important point that can be confusing. Many people do not like their self-image and are eager to form a better one. Obviously, this is a positive desire; however, it presents some difficulties.

What is this better self-image they desire? Do they want an image of themselves that is more confident? Do they want an image that is not so perfect and demanding? Do they want an image that is not so critical and negative? What do they want? Do they know? Most of them probably do not. All they know is that they are dissatisfied with the image they now have of themselves.

The healthiest self-image does not pertain to the idealized or peer

15

group image. Rather, it is the picture of one's self as a real, mature, whole person. We will consider this image further in Chapter Three.

Although much more could be said about your image or ego, I hope enough has been said to help you realize how important it is not to confuse it with the real, mature, whole you. You can see how many negative effects can come from an oversized image. But it is equally important to realize the negative potential of a normal-sized image.

Your image, no matter how positive, is not the real, mature, whole you. It is a mere copy; no copy can compare with the original inside you that is waiting to be developed. The esteem that comes from the real, mature, whole you is preferable to the esteem that comes from others by way of the image they have planted in your head.

* * *

Frank is in his early seventies. Although he is wealthy enough to retire, he continues to work. Work gives him his greatest satisfaction. He proudly tells everyone that he built his business from nothing. Several of his sons and daughters work for him and reap the benefits of his hard labor.

To those who do not live with him, Frank is a very likable person, thoughtful and considerate. To his wife and children, however, Frank is not so likable. It is not that he is cruel; he simply has to have his way in everything. He is judgmental and critical of those who differ from him. He finds fault with the way his wife keeps the house. He insists that his children and grandchildren dress properly for Sunday dinner. His grandson is no longer welcomed to Sunday dinner because he has broken Frank's dress code too many times. "You would not go to a good restaurant that way, would you?" Frank demands.

His oldest son, who works side by side with him, gets the brunt of Frank's criticism. According to Frank, he never does anything right. "I would retire tomorrow if you knew how to carry on," Frank tells him. "But you don't, so I have to stay."

As you might guess, Frank is dominated by his image. He is trying to prove to the world what a great person he is. By constantly putting down his wife and children, he is trying to convince himself of his superiority and of their need of him.

Frank could use an image shrinking. It would be beneficial for both him and his family. If he became more human and loving, he would not have such a need for their respect. He would have their love.

* * *

1. Do you understand what is meant by the *image you*? Where does it come from? What is your *ego*? What is your *conscience*? How do they differ from the image you?
2. What are the positive points of the image you?
3. What are the negative points of the image you?
4. How do you feel when your image is under attack? Are you ready to attack back? Do you run away from what is challenging and embarrassing? Do you brood and obsess when your image is torn? Do you make all kinds of excuses to justify having made a mistake?
5. Do you depend totally on the appraisal of others for your self-esteem? Are you a people-pleaser?
6. What are some ways of detecting the presence and influence of your image?
7. Does this consideration of your image help you understand yourself a little better?
8. What do you think about Frank? Do you know someone like him? Are you like him?

2. THE FEELING YOU

Having looked at the great influence your image can have on your self-esteem, we now ask, "What influence do feelings have on self-esteem?" Before we can answer this question, however, we have to take a quick look at how feelings work and the influence they can have on you.

HOW FEELINGS WORK

Your feelings are a group of magnetic forces inside you that pull you toward what is pleasurable and away from what is unpleasurable. They also tell you what is fair and unfair.

An important question to answer is "What influence do your feelings have upon you?" The answer depends on your state of development. If you are immature, your feelings are everything. How you feel is how you will act. If you are mature, your feelings can add color, power, and excitement to your life; but they will not be allowed to have the final say in decision making. Your intellect and will power will be brought into play to make their judgments about the right and wrong and the goodness of what your feelings want to do.

Your feelings are like the child part of you. They are wonderful to have, but they are not capable of making judgments higher than what is pleasurable or unpleasurable and what is fair or unfair. Feelings should defer to the grownup parts of you. Your intellect and will power should make the final decisions.

MATURITY AND SELF-ESTEEM

To further answer the question about the influence of feelings on self-esteem, we must return again to your stage of maturity.

If you are immature and controlled by your feelings, your feelings greatly influence your self-esteem. Immature people allow their image to determine their worth as human beings. No matter what their intellect tells them, their feelings will choose to accept the verdict of their image over their common sense. They might argue with themselves and say, "I know I should not let what others say run my life, but I can't help it. I can't turn off the voices in my head that tell me how stupid I am when I do something different from others."

If you are mature and in control of your feelings, your feelings will have less control over your self-esteem, because you will listen to them and learn from them, but you will not let them control you.

You can learn a great deal from your feelings that will be valuable for your self-esteem. Your feelings are concerned with pleasure and pain. Now, pleasure and pain have been attached to vital functions to make sure these functions work correctly. The pleasure attached to a vital function attracts you to perform it. The pain you feel comes from not performing it or not performing it correctly. Take as an example the pleasure attached to food. God and nature attached such pleasure to make sure you eat and survive. Not to eat or to eat incorrectly results in pain.

What does this have to do with self-esteem? If you consistently feel good about yourself and what you have done, you have probably acted skillfully and in harmony with your deepest values. On the other hand, if you consistently feel bad about yourself and what you have done, your discomfort and self-blame probably result from behavior that does not reflect your deepest values.

In both cases, I use the word *probably* because, ultimately, feelings are not a totally accurate basis upon which to judge your actions. Although feelings can contribute greatly to your self-esteem, just how valuable that contribution is depends on your maturity as a person. We will consider maturity in Chapter Three.

* * *

Although she is in her early fifties, Dorothy often feels twelve years old. She is constantly in search of attention and will do almost anything to win the acceptance of others. Since she has never thought much of herself, she relies on others to make her feel good about herself.

Does Dorothy act this way because she is stupid? By no means. When not starved for attention, Dorothy is a very intelligent woman who has managed her two careers exceptionally well. Not only is she married with five grown children, she has risen to the top of her profession.

Recently, however, Dorothy found herself in some real turmoil. She has fallen in love with one of her clients. He is handsome, intelligent, and twenty years younger than Dorothy.

Dorothy does not know how to contain herself. Everything inside of her is bursting. She has never felt so good about herself. That someone so much younger considers her beautiful and exciting to be with has sent her self-esteem to an all-time high. *Am I silly to be so content with myself?* she wonders. *Should I dismiss my desires as deluded dreams? If I do, some of my feelings that have finally come alive will die. What a bummer life is!*

Some parts of Dorothy's image are flattered; others are condemning her for acting immaturely. What is she to do? She would do well to read and digest the next chapter before deciding on any course of action.

* * *

1. How well do you understand the workings of your feelings? What are your feelings mostly interested in?
2. Would human life be human without feelings? Why not?
3. What roles do feelings play in an immature person's life? in a mature person's life?
4. What contributions, positive or negative, do your feelings make to your sense of self-esteem and worth?
5. What would you advise Dorothy to do?

3. THE WHOLE YOU

Having considered the influence your image and your feelings can have on your self-esteem, we are ready for the major consideration of this booklet: the highest and best kind of self-esteem you can have. It is a judgment of your worth that is not based on what others say or on what a part of you says. It is a realistic, mature judgment coming from the real, mature, whole you. The following illustration should help you understand this concept.

Imagine yourself standing on the sidewalk of a busy street. From your vantage point at the curb, you notice the cars and trucks speeding by. You may or may not *want* to pay attention to them. If you decide to cross the street, you will have to give them enough attention to decide whether or not it is safe to cross. As long as you choose to stay on the curb, however, you do not have to make a big fuss over the vehicles passing by.

The whole you operates like that. From the moment you awaken in the morning, you can become aware of a stream of consciousness. Slowly, very slowly for some, you can become attuned to the reports of your senses, appetites, feelings, mind, and will power, as well as the dos and don'ts of your image or ego.

What makes you aware of these things is a you that is more than any of them. It is a you that is like a mother hen watching all her chicks pass by. It is the *whole you* on the curb or bank of the stream of your consciousness that receives these reports.

Conscious Choice

How much attention or consideration you will give to these reports should depend on this whole you. Obviously, it will not depend on this whole you if you do not realize that such a you exists. If you identify only with what comes into your head or passes through your attention, then the part of you that screams the loudest in making its reports will be what you are. That part will dominate and take over control. For all practical purposes, it will be you.

The more you realize that you can stand on the curb of your conscious flow and supervise what flows by, not allowing any part to dominate you, the more the whole you will be in control. You will listen to the reports of each part, but the whole you, not the partial you, will decide whether the report is worth acting on or not.

Should you consciously choose to act on a "do" or "don't" of the image you or on a fear or anger report of your feelings, then that action becomes the action of the whole you. By making this conscious choice, you avoid losing a sense of yourself and becoming a slave to your action. It becomes your action for as long as you choose to act on it. If you choose not to act on it, you can do that, too.

Can you picture yourself remaining on the curb of your consciousness and doing the choosing? If you can, you have a picture of the real, mature, whole you. It is real because it comes from you, not others. It is mature because it judges on the basis of what is good for you as a whole person and not on the whim or want of a part of you.

Who Is Going to Win?

A personal example might throw more light on the concept of the whole you. A few years ago I decided to lose twenty pounds. I asked myself, *Who is going to win here? Am I, the whole person, going to win or is a part of me, my appetite for food, going to win?*

I was determined that I would win. I cut down on unnecessary food. Within a month, I lost the twenty pounds. When my appetite for food, especially for tempting desserts, acted up, I repeated my question, *Who is going to win?*

I was going to win.

To help my determination, I reached inside myself for some anger power. I would make a fist with one hand and pound it a number of times into the palm of my other hand. I would do this until I could feel the anger determination take hold of me. It felt like the anger was crawling up my spine.

It worked. The victory was important to me because I lost the weight I did not want or need. But even more important, it helped me be more aware of myself as a whole person.

You also are capable of being a whole person. You can be more than your hunger or feelings. You can decide whether you will act on the reports of your individual parts or not. This whole you is the greatest gift God has given you on the natural level.

GOD'S PLAN

To further help yourself grasp the idea of the whole you, go back to your eternal beginnings. Long before your parents conceived you, God conceived you. God conceived you as a whole person, not in parts. God packed the picture of the whole you into the small container of flesh that began you at your human conception.

Your lifetime work is to unpack this whole you, and it has to be done in stages. The first stage involves your physical birth. The second stage involves your emotional birth, when your feelings are developed or mature enough to cope with a variety of life's situations. The third stage involves your rational, spiritual birth, when you come to the use of reason and free will. At this stage, you can begin to separate yourself from the control of your appetites and feelings and begin to see things as true and good.

In the plan of God, then, your main work is to arrive at an awareness of the whole person God has designed you to be. With good health, encouraging support, helpful examples from others, and your own efforts, you should arrive at some awareness of the whole you in your mid twenties.

Unfortunately, many people never arrive at this awareness or development, for it is not an automatic happening. It has to be worked at. Some people discover and develop individual talents, but they do not arrive at the full picture God conceived them to be. Since human beings cannot be really content until they arrive at a full awareness of their whole selves, it is worth every effort to do so.

SOME QUESTIONS

"Let me get this clear," you may ask, "are you saying that I am capable of standing on the curb or the edge of my consciousness, that I can observe what is flowing by, and that I can remain there and not give in to the reports of my appetites or fears? And are you also telling me that this whole 'I' exists whether something is passing by or not?"

The answer to all of these questions is "yes." You are on the bank of your consciousness before anything passes by, and you can remain there after the different parts of you have made their reports. You can retain the controlling power in a situation.

"I can't believe what you are saying," you might object. "Do you mean that I do not have to act when I become frightened? My fear is telling me in no uncertain terms that I am in danger. Do you mean that I do not have to listen to it?"

No, unless it is the repetition of silly or exaggerated fear, you *should* listen to it. But you should also decide whether it is worth acting on. If you choose not to act on it, then you should turn on your constructive anger and hold your ground. Actually or mentally punch the fist of your one hand into the palm of your other hand and ask, "Who is going to win here? Am I going to win or my fear?" You have the power to win.

"But I *always* give into my fears," you go on. "I do not know how *not* to give into them. The truth is, I feel like I am nothing but fears. I am a bundle of nerves. Can I be different?"

Yes, you can be different.

Practice picturing yourself on the bank of your conscious flow. Now a fear as big as a tidal wave is coming at you. It might be the

24

fear of death or financial loss or some big embarrassment. What are you going to do? run away? stand and fight? just stand and hold your ground?

The best thing to do is to turn on your constructive anger and tell yourself, "I am not going to give in. I am not going to give in."

At first, the words will come as a whisper that cannot be heard above the roar of your fear. Repeat them enough times, though, and they will become stronger. After a while, your fears will recognize that you are not a pushover. More importantly, you will realize that you have some backbone. You are you. You are not fear.

Try it the next time you are afraid and do not want to give in to the fear. Eventually, it will click. When it does, you will feel how much power you have within you.

Some Differences

Since this way of looking at yourself is probably not yet clear because it is so new to you, it will be wise to pause here and look at what we are presenting from a number of angles.

First, how does the whole you differ from the part that identifies with your image? Your image stands back, watches, and decides what you should do. The whole you also stands back, watches, and decides what you should do. So what is the basic difference?

Your image makes its decisions based on the "dos and don'ts" of others. Although it has taken up residence in your memory, it is still exterior, an outsider's decision. It is all prepackaged. It tells you what to do.

The whole you makes decisions based on what is best for you as a whole person. It is not something imposed from the outside. It is interior, springing from deep wells of your being. It is coming from you, and you are making your judgment based on the information you have at the time. The whole you is an awareness you can discover as you step back and realize that the parts of you are just that—*parts of you.* No one part is or should be allowed to be you.

Your image, to be sure, can provide valuable information that should not be taken lightly. Still, the whole you needs to judge whether what has been imposed by others is really for your good as a person. If it is, then you can make it your own and act on it. Having digested it and found it beneficial, you would be a fool not to act on it.

There are other radical differences between the whole you and the image you. The way the two act as your conscience helps make their differences clearer.

YOUR CONSCIENCE—MATURE OR IMMATURE?

A great benefit of discovering and developing the whole you is a mature conscience. Your conscience deals with both the negative and positive aspects of your actions and, consequently, of you the person. It tells you what is morally right or wrong. It urges you to do right and rewards you with peace and contentment when you do. It warns you against doing wrong and punishes you with guilt and remorse when you do what you know is wrong.

For most people, their conscience is their image, composed of the "dos and don'ts" of their training. If they follow these dictates perfectly, they have a "good" conscience and feel that they are "good." If they do not follow them, they have a "bad" conscience, and feel that they are "bad." If these "dos and don'ts" are joined to religion, not only those who implanted them, but God as well gives "good" or "bad" verdicts about one's actions and self-worth.

Yet it should not be too difficult to see that the conscience that results from such training is an immature conscience. It is the conscience of a child, which needs someone in authority to tell the person what to do or not to do. Usually, it is backed up with the reward or punishment of giving or withholding love.

Is such a conscience bad? No, it is merely immature. It should give way to the more mature conscience that the whole-person approach can give. Standing on the bank of your awareness and judging your actions with the measuring stick of *What is good for me as a whole person, and what will help me to live responsibly with others and God?* is a more personal, dependable guide.

So, to eat, drink, or do anything that will hurt you as a person is morally wrong. To disregard the dignity and rights of others is morally wrong. To withhold the love and respect that is due to God is morally wrong.

Perhaps the best conscience is one that consults the "dos and don'ts" of your training but allows the whole you to make the final decision. Such a conscience is priceless. It is an important side of the coin of happiness. A mature love is the other side. In a profound way, these two are joined.

The Masterpiece

The whole you, then, is not the picture or image others want you to be. It is not the many parts that make up you. The whole you is you viewing all the parts of you and the image others have imposed on you. It is you standing on the bank of your awareness and judging, acting, or refusing to act on the reports of the many parts of the image you.

When you are asked, "Who are you? Who are you capable of being?" your answer could and should be "I am the one who is aware, in charge and in control of all of me." This is you, the masterpiece. You are a masterpiece (a piece created by a master) because you were designed and created by the greatest of all masters—God.

Like all great masters, God took a mental picture of you and transmitted it into the seed provided by your parents. To obtain this special picture of you, it is as if God uses a small camera to take self-portraits from many viewpoints. Each of the resulting "snapshots" is a picture of God. One of them is a picture of you. No wonder, then, that you are a masterpiece. You are a piece *of* the master. You are a picture of God.

Does not your awareness of this truth fill you with wonder? Does it not prompt you to want to go on to discover and develop this wonder? How priceless you are if you work out the wonder you are capable of being! You are not a thing; you are a person. There will never ever be another just like you. You are one-of-a-kind.

Many marvelous things could be said about this whole-person

approach to your life. However, we are concerned here with the wholesome effects it can have on your self-esteem. The whole-person approach to life leads to a realistic, mature, and reliable self-esteem—the best kind.

If self-esteem is the judgment you make about your worth, what better judgment can you make than to stand back far enough to make an accurate judgment about your assets and liabilities?

If you make your judgment based on the "dos and don'ts" others have formed in you (your image), you might be standing back too far to form an accurate judgment about your worth. You might be looking at yourself from the distance of childhood when the "dos and don'ts" were imposed.

If you make your judgment based on your feelings, you might not be standing back far enough. Your feelings can be quite nearsighted. They are so concerned about your comfort that they lose sight of you as a whole person.

Therefore, the best kind of approval of yourself comes when you stand on the bank of your consciousness and receive the reports of all the parts of you. From that position, you can get the most accurate picture of yourself. You will not be denying your weak points nor will you be exaggerating your strong points. You will have a clear view of all that pertains to you and others. You will be in a position where you can exercise wisdom.

For our purposes, we can define *wisdom* as the ability to stand back and see things from a proper distance.

What can give you that proper distance?

Prayer can help. It can lift you to the shores of eternity, where you get a better perspective of earth and earthly living. From there, you see more clearly what really counts. The motto of the saints was "How is this going to profit me in eternity?" If it would not profit them in eternity, they did not do it.

Closer to earth, standing on the bank of your awareness is valuable for finding perspective. You are wise to ask yourself, "What is good for me as a whole person?"

Judging yourself from a whole-person approach, you can trust your judgment about your worth as a person and as someone who relates to others as persons. If at times, your judgment proves incorrect, it has the tendency to correct itself. You are too open to life and to yourself to deceive yourself for any length of time.

Continued self-deceit indicates that you have ceased to stand on the bank of your consciousness and judge from there. Of course, combining the proper distancing with prayer reinforces your judgment about yourself and your worth as a person.

* * *

As a child, Donald, now in his late forties, was an honor student. Everyone praised him for his intelligence. His classmates called him "the Brain." Although it had some drawbacks, Donald liked the self-esteem he got from teachers, his parents, and his peers. While trying not to show it, Donald felt superior to others.

Things went well for Donald as he grew into adulthood. He married well, was a regular churchgoer, and had a good business. Then came a severe economic recession. Donald told himself, a little smugly, that he could work things out. Others might fail and fall, but he would be okay.

Donald was not able to work things out, however. He lost his business, his home, and his pride. His image was shattered. His feelings became numb from worry, and he slid into a severe depression. He finally had to admit that he could not work things out. He needed help.

Slowly, Donald was able to slide down from the heights of his intellect and superior image. From a more lowly inward position, he could view his intellect as merely a part of him. He was also able to view his other parts as parts. Gradually, Donald began to be aware of himself as a totality, as a whole person. He refused to let his panic overpower him. He called on his constructive anger to sustain him in his difficulties.

Donald was not sure what to do about his finances and career, but he felt confident he would find a way to cope. He took a job as a waiter in a restaurant and began to plan from there. He felt it was

29

time he served others instead of expecting others always to serve him.

* * *

1. Have you ever stopped to think about what it means to be a real, mature, whole person? Have you acted as if the image you was who you are or should be?
2. Can you picture yourself standing on the curb of your conscious flow? Try it. Let everything—the reports of your senses, appetites, feelings—flow by before you. Can you see yourself as different from all of these reports?
3. Do you understand the difference between a mature conscience and an immature conscience? Which do you think you have?
4. How free are you? Are you really free or are you overinfluenced by your image or your feelings? Are they in control of you or are *you* in control of you?
5. What is wisdom? Are you wise in making judgment?
6. In what ways are you a masterpiece? Is there still work to be done on your personality before the masterpiece can shine through?
7. Can you see why the verdict about yourself that comes from you as a whole person is the most realistic, mature, and reliable self-esteem you can have?

4. WHO'S IN CONTROL?

Before proceeding further, let's take a look at the different sources of self-esteem we have been considering. The questions listed with each section will help you assess the extent of the control exerted by your image, your feelings, and the whole you. Take the time to answer these questions as honestly and thoughtfully as you can. They are important enough to require your best efforts. The answers could steer you in a different direction in regard to your self-esteem and your personality development.

Is Your Image in Control?

Your image can manifest itself in two different ways. It can be outgoing or withdrawing.

Outgoing

- Are you a people-pleaser?
- Do you always seek the attention of others?
- Are you elated when others say favorable things about you? Are you depressed when they say unfavorable things or ignore you?
- Do you drop names and show off the important people you know?
- Do you always talk about the good or clever things you or your family accomplish?

- Do you laugh off criticism and make a joke of it?
- Do you believe your worth depends primarily on what you accomplish?

Withdrawing

- Do you tend to be shy, isolated, or withdrawn from people?
- Do you say very little about yourself because you are afraid of revealing your weaknesses?
- Do you cover up your mistakes with excuses or lies?
- Do you shrink away from criticism?
- Are you unwilling to assert yourself because you cannot risk rejection or failure?
- Do you try to win the sympathy of others by putting yourself down, apologizing profusely, or calling yourself names?
- Do you procrastinate in making decisions?
- Are you a professional dreamer, always hoping things will work out without working on them to make them work out?

If you answered yes to any of these questions, whether on the outgoing or the withdrawing side, you are heavily influenced, if not dominated, by your image. Consequently, your self-esteem will be seriously influenced by other people.

Are Your Feelings in Control?

The following questions will help you to see if or when your feelings control you.

- Do you only do what you feel like doing?
- Are you crushed when others are not sensitive to your feelings?
- Do you unnecessarily cut corners in doing things? Do you make excuses for not making the necessary efforts to keep up with relationships.
- Do you neglect your health because you are afraid to go to doctors or dentists?
- Do you excuse your overindulgence in food by saying you put on weight by just looking at food?

- Do you refrain from church attendance by telling yourself that the sermons are boring and that the church is only interested in money?
- Do you tell yourself that you should go easy on yourself because you have had such a hard life? Are you preoccupied with the unfairness of life?
- Do you pretend not to see things that should be done?
- Do you like to point out the faults of others but are destroyed if they point out your faults?
- Do you tell yourself that your angry outbursts are justified because others provoked you?

A yes to any of these questions indicates that your feelings are dominating you and your self-esteem.

Is the Whole You in Control?

The following questions will help you to see if or when the whole you is in control.

- When faced with the demands of an appetite or a feeling, can you listen and act on the basis of what is best for you as a whole person?
- When faced with a criticism, can you let it register and then decide whether it has any validity to it?
- Do you prefer to know the truth about yourself, even if it is painful?
- Can you accept your limitations, mistakes, and failings and learn from them?
- Do you believe that if a thing is worth doing, it is worth doing well?
- Can you be patient with people, even those whom you perceive as nags, bores, complainers, loudmouths, wimps, and worrywarts?
- Can you accept a compliment graciously and humbly?

A yes to these questions indicates that the whole you is in charge.

The whole you, of course, will give a much more reliable and realistic appraisal of your worth or self-esteem than your image or your feelings.

WHO CONTROLS YOU?

What did you learn from taking this questionnaire about what or who controls you and your self-esteem?

- Is your image in control?
- Are your feelings in control?
- Is the whole you in control, at least some of the time?

If your image is in control, what can you do to lessen its power? Can you see it and treat it as an outside influence? Can you stand up to it and stand back from its beatings when you choose not to follow it exactly? Can you appreciate its contributions to you as a person and as a member of society? Can you have a good chuckle at yourself when you see yourself elaborately planning and conniving to win the praise of others and put yourself in the spotlight? Can you get angry when you see how it makes you shy away from anything challenging? Can you liberate yourself from it without destroying it or yourself?

If your feelings are in control, what can you do to lessen their power? Can you see that your feelings are not adequate to the task of directing you maturely? Can you understand that seeking pleasure and avoiding pain is not a sufficient way to act as a human? Can you detect when you are acting as a child and not as an adult? Can you use your constructive anger to hold your ground and not give in to the harmful pressures of your feelings? Can you listen to your feelings and decide whether you choose to act on them or not?

If the whole you is in control at least some of the time, can you improve or increase its influence? Do you understand what it means to see yourself as a whole person and not as your image or parts? Do you realize the power such an approach gives you to be free, to love fully, and to be a responsible human being? If you do, you are truly blessed.

* * *

One of the greatest difficulties in answering questions such as the ones in this chapter is being truthful with yourself. It is not that you will deliberately be dishonest in answering them. No, the difficulty is in recognizing what is at work and in control of you. People who think they know themselves very well often do not really know themselves at all. They confuse their image or feelings for their real, mature self.

For many years, as a young man and a young priest, I thought I knew myself very well. I was often confused about life, God, and love. On the whole, though, I thought I had a good grasp of life. I was so rational and introspective, I would not let anything pass by me or through me without sorting it out and labeling it.

Then one day I attended an intense workshop on a type of therapy that appealed to me. The therapy stressed honesty. As the workshop progressed, the participants were required to meet one another on a level of weakness. We were encouraged to share with the group the worst thing we had ever done.

When my turn came, I mentioned several faults I had. I was being honest, at least *I* thought so. A member of the group who had been in rehabilitation a long time said he felt an uneasiness as I spoke. He was not sure why, whether the fault was in me or in him. He was called out of the group before he had time to elaborate, but his remarks started me thinking. What was he referring to?

I struggled with myself for a number of hours before I had a hint of what the problem might be. I realized that each time I "lowered myself" by admitting a fault or weakness, I added a reason or an excuse for why I had acted that way. I could not simply state the fault or weakness; I had to defend myself to myself and to others. It was as if as soon as I stated a fault, I immediately erased it. That was not the purpose of the workshop.

As the truth of what I had done hit me, I exclaimed to myself, *Oh, my God, I have always acted this way! I could never be wrong. I always had to be right, to be perfect.* I began to review my life. My

35

lectures as a professor, my sermons as a preacher, and the advice I gave as a counselor all had to be perfect. It bothered me terribly if they were not. Criticism was worse than acid. It ate away at me until I could knock it down and eliminate any rational basis for it. I had not realized how much my image controlled me, how much my image was who I was. Now I look back and wonder how I could have been so blind. I no longer ask why or try to defend myself. I simply accept the fact that I was blind and untruthful.

5. ACCEPTING THE WHOLE YOU

Hopefully, after reading Chapter Four, you concluded that the whole you is in control of your self-esteem. If your image or your feelings are in control, you could be headed for trouble, for they are too nearsighted to give you a clear, whole picture of life. They are too quick to reject what is not to their liking.

In this chapter, we will briefly touch on negative feelings, sexuality, pride, and limitations. All of these aspects contribute to you as a whole person. They also influence your self-esteem. A mistaken idea about them and their presence in your life could be costly to a healthy self-esteem.

ACCEPTING NEGATIVE FEELINGS

If you are like most people, you do not like fear, anger, hatred, or jealously. Not only are these feelings distasteful, they can be embarrassing.

Fear has the appearance of weakness. Anger indicates you are out of control. Hatred is ugly. Jealousy speaks of a smallness of character.

What are you to do with these feelings when they appear? Most people deny them or distract themselves from them, for they are not acceptable to the image of a "nice" person. They lower one's self-esteem.

However, the real, mature, whole person does not view these

emotions in that way. Of course, if uncontrolled, these emotions can be harmful; when kept under control, they can be valuable.

Fear warns you of impending danger. Anger enables you to hold on to your convictions. Hatred can spur you to turn away from evil. Jealousy can stimulate you to strive for what others have attained.

SEXUALITY

Another powerful inner force that can present a problem to your self-esteem is sexuality. On one hand, the casual attitude toward sex today is obvious, and sex is a major attraction in the media. Many, especially the young, do not attach a moral aspect to the use of their sexuality. What gives pleasure is good; what does not is bad. On the other hand, their sexuality is a source of shame for many people. They are afraid to feel, think, or talk about sexual matters. Their background, training, and image make them feel that sexual feelings are too embarrassing to bring out into the open.

What constitues a healthy attitude toward sexuality?

First, accept the fact that you are a sexual person. It is sexuality that accounts for many of the male/female differences in human personalities. For this reason, an honest acceptance of sexuality is fundamental.

Having accepted and acknowledged your sexuality, you must allow the whole you to decide on its proper use. The natural question should be, "What is going to be good for me as a whole person? Should I express or not express, use or not use, my sexuality?" If your good demands that you not express or use your sexuality, and your sexual feelings are insistent on having their way, then ask, "Who is going to win here? Am I, the whole person or a part of me going to win?" This is where your anger can act as a backup to your determination that you, not a part of you, is going to win.

Approaching your sexuality this way, you do not have to be embarrassed over its presence and pressures. You can acknowledge to yourself, and if it is profitable, to others that you are very much aware of your sexuality.

There is no need, therefore, for the existence of your sexuality to diminish your self-esteem. To abuse your sexuality or to deny it are both cause for loss of self-esteem, but to recognize it as a vital, dynamic part of you is not. God included sexuality in your personality kit precisely because of its value to the individual and to society.

PRIDE

Another aspect of your life and personality with potential to cause problems is pride. Is it good to be proud or not? Should you accept pride as a part of your personality or reject it? To answer these questions, we need to distinguish between the positive and the negative faces of pride.

The positive face of pride reflects the real, mature, whole you and expresses itself in reasonable, justifiable praise of yourself and your accomplishments. It simply acknowledges that you have been wonderfully made and given special talents by God. When you use these talents wisely and successfully, you can and should give yourself credit. You are following the lead of Jesus, who acknowledged and praised such good use when he said, "Well done, good and trustworthy slave" (Matthew 25:21). By giving due credit to God, you are not only being honest and truthful, you are also giving glory to God.

The negative face of pride comes from an overidealized image of yourself. If you are foolish enough to believe that you are or can be all that such an image wants you to be, you are always in danger of having low self-esteem.

Positive pride, then, is a positive quality. Because it is the truth, it adds to your self-esteem. Negative pride, on the other hand, is a negative quality. Because it is a lie, or at least an exaggeration, it detracts from your self-esteem.

LIMITATIONS

To foster proper self-esteem you need to accept your limitations. The first such limitations come from the fact of your creaturehood. As a creature, you are not only limited, of yourself, you are nothing. Everything you are has been given to you.

The second kind of limitations you need to accept comes as a result of your individuality. As an individual, you may or may not develop all that has been given to you. By way of omission, your life can have numerous empty spaces because you have not lived up to your potential. By way of commission, you have made many mistakes that have impeded your growth as an individual.

Regardless of their source, most people find it difficult to accept their limitations and mistakes. Much of this nonacceptance is a result of negative pride. It comes from the image instilled in you by your training. According to this image, it is not acceptable to fail or make mistakes. It is too embarrassing; only perfection is acceptable.

Some nonacceptance originates with feelings. Because your feelings represent the child part of you, you can find yourself caught up in childish omnipotence. As a child, you liked to imagine that you were all-powerful, that you could do anything. Your childish imagination automatically eliminated any limitations.

The real, mature, whole you does not have a problem accepting limitations. It will want you to overcome deficiencies and mistakes that can be corrected, but it can do so humbly and patiently.

Limitations, then, are a part of life. They need not and should not detract from a healthy self-esteem. If you react poorly to limitations, becoming extremely self-critical, they can diminish your sense of worth. They *can*, but they need not be allowed to.

Although there are other unwanted parts and actions, what we have considered here should help you understand and accept your whole self more fully. God has put you together in a marvelous way. Negative aspects of your being balance positive aspects. The best way to keep this balance is to stand on the curb of your consciousness and allow all aspects of yourself to make their reports. It is up to your real, mature, whole personality to choose which parts you will act on. In this way, you are in touch with your total personality and the world outside you. You are in contact with reality. You are the person God made you to be. You are in charge of yourself and of material creation. Realizing this, you can rightly esteem yourself as a wonder, a wonder of God.

* * *

I met Denise many years ago on board the Italian liner that took me to Italy to further my studies. While others were dancing the evening away, I decided to go to the chapel. As I was making the Stations of the Cross, I was distracted by the huddled figure of a young woman deep in prayer. It was Denise.

After I finished the stations, I tapped Denise on the shoulder and said hello. She looked up at me with the friendliness of both a child and a mature adult. From that moment, when we talked and became friends, I was impressed by her graciousness. But only later did I learn what a truly special person Denise was.

I marveled at the way she accepted and balanced her talents and her life. She was proud of her accomplishments, yet she humbly recognized how good God had been to her. She was strong personally and spiritually, yet she was weak physically.

Because rheumatic fever had kept Denise out of regular school as a child, she had private tutors who helped her at home. She was frightened by her poor health, yet she was strong with her angry determination to make use of her talents. Denise was jealous—of the saints. A saintly person herself, she accepted all of life as a challenge from God.

At times when I look back, I wonder if my appraisal of Denise was an exaggerated flight of fantasy. Could anyone be so good, so balanced? Yes, if they have been working at it with determination and love.

* * *

1. Why do people have difficulty accepting themselves? Why do they want to deny, or at least hide, their shortcomings, mistakes, and failures?
2. What do you do when you are afraid? Are you a fear-filled person? Are you in touch with a ready supply of constructive anger to help you hold your ground when you are frightened?
3. Is it unchristian to feel hatred?
4. When is jealousy positive? When is it negative?

5. Are you comfortable with your sexuality? Did your early training encourage you or discourage you from acknowledging sexuality?

6. Are you a proud person? Is that good or bad?

7. Are you a humble person? Can you accept your limitations as a creature and as an individual? Are you willing to face and correct mistakes and failings?

8. Can you accept all of your personality and work with it to arrive at the masterpiece God made you to be?

6. THE HIGHEST FORM OF SELF-ESTEEM

When you recognize yourself as a whole person and accept all of yourself, you are in touch with the highest form of self-esteem. It is more reliable and vastly superior to the esteem of others or of your feelings. It is the best kind of human confidence.

As marvelous as the esteem coming from the real, mature, whole you is in itself, it is especially marvelous when it puts you in a position to respond more fully to the gift of supernatural life.

AN ELEVATED LIFE

It is wonderful to be fully human and alive to all of your humanity. As a human being, you stand as the spokesperson for nature. You can speak for every voiceless creature that exists.

It is even more wonderful to be a human elevated into the intimate life of God. Through the greatness of God and the generosity of Jesus, you have been called to a life that is very much like divine life. By way of belief, water, and the Holy Spirit, you are invited into a life that is divine. Because it is a gift freely given, it is called the life of grace.

Are you aware of this higher form of life? If you are and if you can surrender your whole self to it, this surrender grafts you into God and God is grafted into you. Your actions are no longer only human; they flow with divine life and power. You now choose on the basis of what will be healthy for you as a whole person who has been elevated to the divine. Your dignity and self-worth are beyond calculating.

"But how can I take esteem from a gift that is freely given to me?" you may ask. "I did not earn it." To take advantage of the esteem that comes from God's gift, you must understand that esteem comes from two sources. It comes from who and what you are and from what you do with what you have. Most people esteem themselves only on the basis of what they do and not on who they are. This is unfortunate, because both are valuable sources of self-esteem. Realizing that you are the possessor and participator in divine life should boost your stock immensely.

GOD KNOWS YOUR WORTH

Although the most satisfying self-esteem comes from within yourself rather than from others, when the other is God, this evaluation of your worth is extremely valuable. What does God say about your worth and how you should feel about yourself?

God says, "You are my masterpiece. I have thought of you and loved you with an eternal love. I have equipped you with marvelous qualities. I have made you according to my own image and likeness. Besides, I have sent my Son to tell you what I think of you. He did this most convincingly from Calvary. The cross was the price tag of your worth. That is how much I love you and value you." God has given you the best—the divine Self and yourself.

On your part, you would do well to learn the "standing back" procedure. Stand back on the bank of your consciousness and see yourself as a whole person. Also, take yourself to the shores of eternity and judge yourself, and things outside yourself, from that distance. The saints used this most helpful technique, judging everything from the distance of eternal shores. When they were about to speak or act, they asked themselves, *How is what I am about to do or say going to help in eternal life?* If it would not be helpful, they did not do or say it.

The capacity to stand back and view yourself and the things of earth from a proper distance is the essence of wisdom. Standing too close to your parts and the things of earth is foolishness, not wisdom.

SOIL AND SEED

The most fertile ground for self-esteem, then, is a healthy, natural, whole approach to yourself combined with surrender to the supernatural gift that elevates you and allows you to participate in God's power and life. Do you understand this winning combination? The parable Jesus told about the sower and the seed illustrates it perfectly.

To show how we must cooperate with the actions of God, Jesus compares the Father to a farmer who sprinkles seed on the ground. Some seed falls by the wayside, some on rocky ground, some among thorns, some on good ground. How much fruit the seed will produce depends not only on the seed but on the ground. If the ground is receptive, the results will be good; otherwise, the results will be disappointing. (See Matthew 13:3-9.)

The same is true of the call to a higher-than-human life. The results do not depend on the call but on the development, the quality of the ground, of the human life that receives it. If that life is not sufficiently developed, the call will die out like the seed that fell on rocky, scorched, or thorny soil. It failed to produce its potential.

The best way to develop the ground of your life is to be in control of yourself as a real, mature, whole person. Then you are capable of responding to the call. You are capable of being elevated. As in the parable, when the ground of your life is rich, you are capable of living and loving to a thirtyfold, sixtyfold, or hundredfold amount.

On the other hand, if instead of the rich, receptive ground of a whole person, you present the ground of the image you, the call will not be as effective. Your image will try too hard to fit this call into the structures of your training. That is what the Jewish leaders did when they condemned Jesus for curing on the Sabbath. Jesus countered that the Sabbath, which was good, was made for humans and therefore must give way when it interferes with what is humanly good.

Nor is a ground based upon feelings capable of understanding God's lofty call. The judgments of your feelings, based on pleasure and pain, are often too immature and shaky to sustain all the good prepared for those who love God.

RESTORATION OF SELF-ESTEEM

Although we have been mainly concerned in this booklet with the awareness and development of self-esteem, it is important to give some consideration to the loss of self-esteem that results when humans act contrary to their dignity as people called in a special way to union with God. In other words, we need now to talk about sin.

What is sin?

Most people think that sin is breaking a moral law or commandment. They may say, for example, "I sinned because I broke the sixth commandment." Such a statement gives the impression that if the behavior in question did not break a commandment—something forbidden by God—there would be no sin. The fact that it involves a *commandment* makes it wrong.

Of course, in a way this is true. A better approach to sin, however, is to realize that we sin when we break an *order* that should exist with God, with other people, and within ourselves. A law or commandment simply states what that order is. To break that law or commandment is to be "out of order." Things and people that are out of order do not function properly. Obviously, this is a bad situation.

When you have sinned and are out of order, you lose much of your worth and dignity. Your self-esteem plunges. You feel worthless. You feel you have less worth.

Mending bridges

How can you restore your worth? If you are out of order with others, you can try to restore the right order. You can mend the rift by owning up to your feelings and making amends.

If you are out of order within yourself because you have let one part take control and it has gotten you to do something that goes against your good as a whole person, you can try to return to the bank of your consciousness and take back control of yourself.

If you are out of order with God because of a direct offense against God or by being out of order with others or within yourself, you can ask for forgiveness. You cannot restore a right order with God. Only God, the one offended, can do that. Fortunately, God is always disposed to mend the relationship.

Once all the bridges of your life have been put back into good working order, self-esteem returns. In some ways, it is restored even more substantially than before precisely because you had to make a sincere effort to restore yourself. That in itself is praiseworthy and elevates your worth as a person.

* * *

Caught somewhere between her teens and adulthood, Grace stands as straight and tall as an exclamation mark when she is feeling confident. When she is not so confident, however, she stands curved like a question mark.

Grace is in the process of searching for her deep inner self, where she can be at peace. A shy and introspective person, she has always allowed trivial things to assume great importance. Another person's disagreement could touch her spider-web sensitivities, jolting her to the core of her being.

At first, Grace attributed her supersensitivity to a delicate sense of hurt because she saw people who should be loving not living up to their potential. After a while, however, she realized that her hurt was more personal. She did not know how to cope with insensitive, angry people. They frightened her into inertia; she would become so paralyzed inside she could hardly move away from the hurt. Slowly, she began to realize she needed help.

What a beautiful change solid, sympathetic help has made in Grace's life! She now realizes that the power she had been wasting by denying her anger can be used constructively. She can stand and fight—or just stand and not run away as she had always done in the past.

Slowly, Grace has begun to realize that she is a masterpiece of God. Others might try to destroy her, but they cannot succeed unless she allows them to. She is not going to allow them that power any longer.

As these convictions settled in, they warmed the thermometer of Grace's self-esteem to new heights. She began to accept that she is special. She could not reverse the process even if she wanted to. Her old ways were a dungeon. Her new ways are an open road with no dead ends. Not even death can put a roadblock in the way.

One day, looking at the beauty of a rose, Grace smiled radiantly and told the rose, "You are indeed beautiful, but I am more beautiful. I have been graced beyond your goodness. I am correctly called Grace because I am a free gift of God."

* * *

1. Have you been given God's special invitation to enhance your natural life with supernatural life? Have you appreciated and esteemed both of these gifts? Do you feel better about yourself knowing that you have been so blessed?
2. What is God's appraisal of you and of the things God has given you? How does Jesus appraise your worth? How can God's appraisal of you help your self-esteem?
3. How can you become rich soil for nurturing and developing the gifts God has given you?
4. What is sin? Why is it so bad to be out of order? How can you put things back in order with God, others, and yourself?

7. ACCEPTING THE CHALLENGE

So now you are faced with a challenge. Will you seek the self-esteem that comes from you as a real, mature, whole person or the self-esteem that comes from your image or your feelings?

Obviously, this is an important challenge. If your self-esteem is not based on the steady ground of you, the whole person, it will be built on unsteady ground of the opinion of others or on your feelings, neither of which is a reliable source of self-esteem.

I sincerely hope you have decided to set as a goal the self-esteem that comes from your whole person. This is not an easy way, but it is the most rewarding way. In this chapter, we will consider some of the struggles and rewards that this choice involves.

A CORE STRUGGLE

If you are like most people, you spend some of your thinking time wondering who you really are. At times, you seem to be whatever comes into the conscious flow of your mind. At other times, you feel as if you are all the dos and don'ts of your training and image.

At still other times, you seem to be your feelings. Often, as these different forces attempt to take control of you, a conflict arises. At such times you have to wait to see whether your image, your appetites, or your feelings will run you.

As you try to stand on the bank of your conscious flow of

awareness, a serious tug of war can take place between parts of you and the whole you. If your image has had too much control over you, it will not let go easily. It is set in its ways. Its punishments of anxiety and panic are ready to pounce on you should you fail to live up to its dos and don'ts. If you try to take control, it will fight you with every fear imaginable. This is not a new conflict.

Jesus refers to this conflict when he talks about putting a new piece of cloth on an old garment or putting new wine into an old wineskin. (See Mark 2: 21-22.) Jesus was put to death for trying to introduce some deeper insights into the religion of his time. The religious leaders had him killed rather than change their ways.

Your image was likewise imposed on you when you were very young. It is the old piece of cloth or the old wineskin. Being controlled by your whole self is the new cloth or the new wine. Do not be surprised if a life-and-death struggle breaks out in you. Your image will insist on having the last word. Of course, the challenge is not to allow it to have the final say. The whole you should be the final decider.

The same struggle can occur if your feelings have been in control. They will not let go easily. You will have to do battle with them and not let them win.

PATIENT WAITING

The struggle to be a whole person requires effort, time, and patience to see results in this internal civil war. You need to stay on constant guard. As Jesus said so often, "Stay awake." You do not know when your image or your feelings will try to take control.

It will take patience to become accustomed to standing on the bank of your consciousness. For most people, it is an unfamiliar sensation, more an awareness or a conviction than a feeling. You know when you are there, and you know when you are not. You know when the whole you is in control and when your image or feelings are in control. At times, especially in the beginning, you will tire of having to be so vigilant. You will want to go back to the "good old days" when you were less complicated—or at least thought you were.

When the Jews of the Old Testament were liberated from the slavery of Egypt, they complained that it was better to be a slave than put up with their struggles to find themselves as a nation. (See Exodus 16:2.) So too you will complain that it is too hard to find the whole you. That is okay; it will pass. The struggle will lessen. In the meantime, be patient and remain on guard.

A sense of humor helps tremendously. As you become more nervous and stressed, think of the two dreams the patient brought to his psychiatrist. "Doctor, I have these two recurring dreams. In one, I am a tepee; in the other, I am a wigwam. What does it mean?" The doctor replied, "It means that you are two tents (too tense)."

Speaking of doctors and patience, where would a doctor be without patients? A sense of humor can help you not to take yourself too seriously. The image you can be very serious. It can make life sound so hard, especially if you had negative, complaining parents. A sense of humor can help you see your pain as birth pains or growing pains.

If you hang on during the dark of storms and struggles, you will see the light of dawn. With the dawn comes a beautiful sunrise. At least, this has been my experience in dealing with myself and with others. I have tried to capture this struggle and its darkness and in a poem that you might find appropriate to your situation.

"Fear Not the Fog's Thickness"
Behind each task,
faced with appropriate mask,
was a little girl who knew
how to say what was expected,
and how not to be rejected.
She was a furnace without fire,
A dream without real desire.
She had so much to know,
so much for show,
so little for self,
        lost somewhere on a shelf.

Where it really counts,
in adding up the amounts
   of her that is still to be,
she is like a cup before the sea.
I fear and fear not
   for her future lot.
It will come through
   with the good and true,
of that I am sure,
   and it will endure.
Your head shakes no.
You cannot grow.
You are too tired.
Too little fired.
Confuse not the feeling
   with the pain of peeling
   the outer wrapping
   from the inner happening.
Fear not the fog's thickness.
Emerging is an inner richness—
   You.

THE REWARDS

We have glimpsed the rewards that come from basing worth and
self-esteem on the discovery and development of the real, mature,
whole you. We will reiterate a few of those rewards here.

You are rewarded when you avoid the shortcomings of basing
your self-esteem on your image or feelings. Your image tends to
make you a people-pleaser. You are not your own person. You are
not real.

Your feelings tend to keep you pleasure-bound. You are a
pleasure-seeker, a pain-avoider. You are not interested in people as
individuals, only in how they can help you. You are immature. Your
self-esteem goes up or down depending on others or on what gives
you pleasure. Neither is dependable.

A more positive set of rewards comes with the knowledge that your self-esteem is not based on fantasy but on reality. You can trust it. You can build on it. You know what talents you have, and you can be satisfied with them. You derive joy when you use your talents correctly. Your use of talents, not the results, is important, and you are happy regardless of the results. You are happy whether other people approve or disapprove of their use.

Perhaps the greatest reward of such self-esteem is that it produces a healthy love of yourself. The more you see yourself as a totality, as the masterpiece God made you to be, the more you love what God has given you. You realize that you are unique because you have been so marvelously made. You are a one-of-a-kind wonder.

From this solid base of self-esteem and self-love, you are capable of reaching out to everyone and accepting what they have to offer. You are not afraid of them or their rejection. You are willing to share as much of yourself as they are capable of receiving.

Once you achieve this kind of self-esteem based on the real, mature, whole you, the rewards are many. As Jesus would say, "The fields are ripe for harvest."

* * *

Joe was one of six children. He always wanted to be the center of attention and would do anything to put himself there. He would play the clown, make fun of himself, and do crazy things. Everyone told him he should be on the stage, and he would laugh and say that the stage left before he got there.

When Joe reached his thirties, his parents began to worry about him because he would not take anything seriously. They didn't like the late hours he kept or his inability to hold a job or to maintain a relationship with a woman. On top of everything else, they suspected that he drank too much.

One day, Joe was in a serious car accident. Although not drunk, he had been drinking. Although the police officer who arrived on the scene realized the state Joe was in, he did not arrest him. Knowing his parents and family, the police officer took Joe home and warned his parents that Joe needed counseling. They agreed. Reluctantly, so did Joe.

After Joe admitted that he always needed to be the center of attention, Joe's therapist asked if he had a brother or sister just a little younger. Joe replied that his sister was a year younger.

"Wow," the therapist exclaimed, "that means you only had a few months of narcissistic time where you were the center of attention. Every child needs at least two years of narcissistic time. If he does not get it then or make up for it later by way of the intense 'in-love' experience, which lasts about two years, he will crave for it the rest of his life."

Joe's eyes lit up. "I didn't realize that," he said. That explains a lot. Here I thought the important question in regard to birth was 'Who came first, the chicken or the egg?' Now I see how important the shell is. There is no yolking about it." He laughed heartily at his own corny joke.

The therapist laughed, too, and realized that Joe would be a good candidate for therapy. His sense of humor could help him stand back from his image and parts and their seriousness in having their own way. It could also help him not give up when the going got rough. The therapist felt that Joe had made up his mind to accept the challenges of reality, especially the reality about himself and his capabilities to be a whole person.

* * *

1. Have you accepted the challenge to be a real, mature, whole person?
2. Is there a struggle within you? What happens if you do not do what your image says? What happens if you do not do what your feelings say?
3. Have you ever felt a fog within yourself so that you could not see clearly where to go or what to do?
4. Do you have a sense of humor? Can you use it to bring a ray of sunshine when you are in a fog because of your inner struggles?

8. WHEN YOU NEED HELP

At this point, a few suggestions might help you obtain the full benefits of this booklet. Do not be discouraged if you have not immediately grasped all of its contents. Not only have we been dealing with a heavy subject, we have had to deal with it in a highly concentrated form to keep it from expanding into several volumes. As with concentrated juices, this booklet might be too strong to take all at once or alone. You might need to reread it several times, and you might need some help to digest it. Some people approach difficult tasks better with the help of another. This chapter will give some practical advice on choosing someone to help you should you feel a need for it.

CHOOSING A GUIDE

The most important quality to look for when choosing a guide is personal experience. Choose someone who has instructed others in this process to help you discover and develop the real, mature, whole you and the self-esteem it brings.

Personal experience

Here are some questions to ask regarding your potential guide's personal experience in the process of self-discovery. (We are using the feminine pronoun for smoother reading, but of course, the same criteria hold for either a male or a female guide.)

- How well does she conduct her own life?
- Is she confident?
- Is she attuned to all of life?
- Does she have self-discipline and control?
- Does her image appear to be in its proper place as a consultant and not as the director of her personality?
- Does she have worthwhile goals?
- Is she a happy person?

Instructional experience

You can judge her capability to guide and instruct others in this process by her sensitivity and commitment to relationships.

Often, the person seeking help is like a lost child. Despite his outward appearance, he has no sense of self-worth. He functions, but he does not feel. He is looking for unconditional love. He needs to know he will not be condemned or abandoned because he has said or done something stupid, for he is already overloaded with negatives. He does not need to be reprimanded for his stupidity, for his image beats him into a pulp with questions and accusations. He needs to be reassured by his guide that mistakes are not the end of the world and that it is better to do something poorly than not to do it at all. He needs someone to teach him how to be positive about himself and his life. He needs someone to prime the pump of positives that lie so deeply buried inside that he never feels them.

Obviously, the more experienced and capable your guide, the better your chances of succeeding in your search for the whole you and its solid self-esteem.

WHERE TO LOOK

After considering the qualities of a good guide, the question arises, "Where can I find such a capable person?" The discovery of someone in touch with her whole self and capable of communicating her discovery to others is not an easy task. You might have to shop around.

The first place to look is among your circle of acquaintances, seeking out someone you feel has the qualities of mature self-esteem you desire. It could be a friend, a cowork, a leader in your church or in the community. If you find after a while that the person you have chosen does not seem to be acting from her whole self but from an image that is impressive but not deep, keep looking until you find someone who has achieved or is achieving the fuller aspects of her personality.

Perhaps you will decide to seek a professional guide. She could be a psychologist, a psychiatrist, a counselor, or other mental-health specialist. Ask friends to recommend professionals with whom they have worked. Or you might choose a pastoral counselor or a member of the clergy who has studied counseling.

Help is available. As Jesus would say, "Ask, and it will be given you; search and you will find; knock, and the door will be opened for you" (Matthew 7:7).

GOD AS GUIDE

You are overlooking a valuable source of help in the search for the real, mature, whole you, if you fail to consider God as a guide. Whether you realize it or not, your pull in life is toward God as the only one capable of quieting your will's restless longing for goodness. God alone can fill your bottomless human heart. God is the ultimate love object, the main reason for your desire to find your whole self. Invited to a relationship with the Divine, you want to be yourself at your best. You do not want to relate to God by way of substitutes. God is the one reality that explains all other realities.

Nor is the deep longing only on your part. God wants to be active in your life. Jesus glories in being the "good shepherd." He says, "I am the good shepherd, I know my own and my own know me, just as the Father knows me and I know the Father" (John 10:14-15).

Jesus wants the deepest possible relationship with you. He calls you friend. (See John 15:15.) He invites you to come to him if you need help, and he promises not to turn away. (See Matthew 11:28.) He wants to be with you, in you, whether you need help or not. (See John 14:23.)

In addition to the help and companionship God offers you in your search for the whole you, Jesus offers you an example of what it is like to live as a whole person. He does not act from "image." He respects the past, but he is his own person. He will not do things just to please or impress others. Those who do that, he says, already have their reward. (See Matthew 6:1-2.) He is not ambitious to promote himself but says, "Whoever wishes to become great among you must be your servant; and whoever wishes to be first among you must be slave of all" (Mark 10:43-44). Nor does he avoid doing what is right because others will disapprove. Eventually, of course, this will bring about his death.

Obviously, Jesus is in control of himself. He will not let parts of himself run him. He would rather be without those parts than have them control him. He says that if your right eye is an occasion of sin, cast it out. He says the same about your hand. (See Matthew 5:29-30.) Nor will he let fear or anxiety control him. (See Matthew 6:25-34.) Jesus based his judgments upon what would be good for him as a whole person who loved his Father and who loved others. His love would prompt him to give his life to and for them.

UNDERSTANDING THE WAYS OF GOD

Although many would want God as their guide in discovering and developing their whole personalities, they do not know how to make meaningful contact. They may have tried to make contact with God in other areas where they needed help. Receiving no answer, however, and not understanding the reason for this, they stopped trying after a while.

In seeking to contact God to be a guide in pursuing the whole you, there are a couple of important points to remember.

You have a friend

God is a good listener, always available for consultation. You do not have to schedule an appointment. While you might not receive a direct reply, God is listening and is sympathetic. God will listen as often and as long as you call, like a loving Parent.

58

Obviously, it is extremely valuable to know that someone cares enough to really listen to you. It helps you air out your feelings or your problem. It helps to take away some of the pain of loneliness. This is one of the great benefits of having a good friend. Many times, you are not looking for advice but for someone just to be there and listen. In God, you have just such a friend.

Indirect assistance

When you ask God for help, direct assistance may not always be forthcoming. Instead, as a good guide who wants you to use and develop your talents to work out the mystery of your whole self, God provides you with all you need to handle the problem yourself.

Therefore, do not be fooled into believing that God is not helping you because nothing seems to be happening. A great deal is happening; a whole process is beginning. As you face a problem, a common approach is to become frightened and want to run away from it. A better one is to stand back a little and see what can be done about the problem. If it is difficult but manageable, you can work up your constructive anger and not run away. You can put your talents to work to find a solution. If the problem is not manageable alone because it is bigger than you or bigger than human help can provide, then God will step in more directly.

In the case of finding the whole you, most likely you can work it out on your own or with the help of other humans. While this is happening, God watches your every step, providing what you need, waiting, and encouraging. God fills your mind and heart with satisfaction as you take your first baby steps in the direction of discovering and developing the you on the curb of your conscious flow.

It is understandable that you would like God to do more of the actual work of this discovery for you. Try to realize, however, that God is God and sees the whole picture. We often see only part of the picture because we are too close to the situation. After all, God is an experienced guide and has been at the work of helping people find themselves a lot longer than we have.

CONFIDENCE IN YOUR GUIDE

Whether the guide you choose to help you in this venture of finding yourself is human or divine, you need to have confidence in that guide to receive the full benefits of help.

Confidence is the magnetic force that holds you to your guide. The greater your confidence, the greater the attention you will pay to her words and example.

What exactly is confidence? One kind of confidence comes with the knowledge that you have accomplished something successfully a number of times and feel self-assured that you can do it again successfully.

Another kind of confidence is doing something with faith—*cum fide*. What is faith? Faith is accepting a truth from someone you know to be knowledgeable and sincere. You believe that she knows what she is talking about and that she is communicating what she knows honestly. Faith is seeing through your guide's eyes or mind what she has seen with her eyes or mind. You are making her eyes and mind your own. If she says a goal is possible and that there are steps leading toward it, you accept it. You accept it even more strongly if you see she has reached the goal.

Without realizing it, you exercise this confidence in others many times a day. You do it when you accept what newspapers have to say and when you attend classes or go shopping. So you are not unfamiliar with superficial confidence. It probably does not present a problem for you.

DEPTH CONFIDENCE

The kind of superficial confidence described above, however, is not what we mean by having depth confidence in your guide. In the beginning, you might find that trusting or believing in another comes somewhat easily. At last, you have found someone who is really interested in you. She is the answer to a prayer.

After a while, however, this trust may become more difficult. Not only is the going getting rough, but doubts about others you have trusted in the past might be surfacing. You have been disappointed and hurt so many times by people you trusted. After all, your lack of development is not totally your own doing. Parents, friends, teachers, and others have let you down. Somewhere deep inside, you told yourself you would never really trust another again.

This lack of trust is not unusual, and an experienced guide will watch for it and know how to handle it. Her first reaction to your accusations and mistrust will be to examine them to see if they have to do with her own shortcomings. If she finds that they stem from her way of relating to you, she will discuss the matter with you and change what is undesirable. If they have to do with your past or some other factor, she will take them seriously but not personally. She will encourage you to air out what is buried and is still bothering you and will help you deal with it. This will increase your confidence in her.

Confidence in your guide, then, is all-important. It can remove some of the scary aspects of making the journey alone. Moreover, you are more likely to accomplish your goal when you work toward it with the help of an interested and interesting other. Besides accomplishing the goal, you also have someone with whom to share your successes and failures.

*   *   *

Forty-year-old Ginger exudes confidence. This confidence, combined with her personal and mental sharpness, have made her successful in a field dominated by men. She likes to be around her male coworkers, and they like to have her around.

Lately, however, Ginger had not been herself. Was it because her parents moved away? Was it because she is getting older and is still unmarried? Was it because her younger brother recently confided in her that he has AIDS?

Was it this? Was it that? Ginger didn't know, and she was tired of thinking about it. She was just not her usual happy, sharp, confident self.

What could she do? Who could she talk to? She didn't want to burden her friends, nor did she want to go to a professional and admit she needed help. Finally, she decided to get away for a few days. She would go to the shore by herself for the weekend. She would not make any plans. She would simply pack an overnight bag and stop when she was tired of driving or found a place that caught her fancy.

Those were the circumstances that brought Ginger to our retreat house in West End, Long Branch, New Jersey. As she was driving along Ocean Avenue, not sure why, she stopped and rang our bell.

"I was passing by and saw the sign San Alfonso Retreat House," she said. "I wondered what the place was all about."

I welcomed her in and showed her around. As we walked and talked, Ginger hesitated. It was obvious that she had something she wanted to ask me or tell me but did not know whether she should. We sat down in the beautiful South West room with its many windows overlooking the ocean. Within a few moments, she began to empty her burdened heart.

Her fears and pain were contagious. I caught both of them and told her I was sorry she had to go through so much alone. Ginger smiled a rainbow smile—a smile through tears still flowing down her cheeks. "I really have not been through it all alone," she said. "God has been with me and is probably the one who directed me here."

* * *

1. Have you ever felt you needed help to clear away the confusion of your mind? Did you seek help? How did it turn out? What qualities were helpful or hurtful in the guide you chose?
2. How sensitive should a guide be to be effective? How experienced should he or she be?
3. When is the best time to go for help? Should you wait until you cannot bear the burden any more?
4. Have you turned to God for help when you needed it? Did God help you? How?
5. In what ways is Jesus a good example for living totally?
6. What is confidence? How does one gain self-confidence? What does it mean to have confidence in your guide? Why is this so important?

CONCLUSION

It is wise to realize that seeking and discovering yourself as a whole person can never have a conclusion. God made you as an ever-expanding universe. The more you are aware of yourself as a whole person, the more you can be aware of your parts. They pass like a parade before you, the whole person, standing on the curb of your conscious flow.

The more you are aware of yourself as a whole person, the more you can be in control of your parts. They answer to you; you do not answer to them. This awareness of your total self gives you independence. You do not have to lean on others with a crippling dependency, nor do you have to run away from others into an obvious or subtle isolation.

This awareness of yourself gives you the power to open all the doors of your heart to others, no matter where they are in their development. If you encounter others who are also aware of themselves as whole persons, you have fulfilled love's dream. Love wants nothing more than to share a total self with another total self.

So the rewards of seeking and discovering the total self God created you to be are great. Nothing gives you a better self-image and the right kind of self-esteem. Ideally, you realize this somewhere deep inside and will put forth every effort to obtain it.

Many thanks for listening. It has been my happiness to share these treasures about the person you can be. I have found that living according to the truths presented in this booklet has given me the key to great happiness. I sincerely hope it does the same for you.